To Tim   all love,
J   Mom

It has been an honor
to be your mom.

If I were given a chance to be
anything I wanted to become,
there's nothing I would rather be
...than your parent.

And there is no one
I would rather have
...as my son.

— Laurel Atherton

Blue Mountain Arts ®
Bestselling Books

By Susan Polis Schutz:
To My Daughter, with Love, on the Important Things in Life
To My Son, with Love
I Love You

Is It Time to Make a Change?
by Deanna Beisser

To the Love of My Life
by Donna Fargo

100 Things to Always Remember... and One Thing to Never Forget
Chasing Away the Clouds
For You, Just Because You're Very Special to Me
To the One Person I Consider to Be My Soul Mate
by Douglas Pagels

Being a Teen ...Words of Advice from Someone Who's Been There
by Diane Mastromarino

girls rule ...a very special book created especially for girls
by Ashley Rice

A Lifetime of Love ...Poems on the Passages of Life
by Leonard Nimoy

Anthologies:
42 Gifts I'd Like to Give to You
Always Believe in Yourself and Your Dreams
A Daughter Is Forever
For You, My Daughter
Friends for Life
I Love You, Mom
I'm Glad You Are My Sister
The Joys and Challenges of Motherhood
The Language of Recovery ...and Living Life One Day at a Time
Life Can Be Hard Sometimes ...but It's Going to Be Okay
May You Always Have an Angel by Your Side
Take Each Day One Step at a Time
Teaching and Learning Are Lifelong Journeys
These Are the Gifts I'd Like to Give to You
Think Positive Thoughts Every Day
Thoughts to Share with a Wonderful Teenager
To My Child
With God by Your Side ...You Never Have to Be Alone

There Is Greatness Within You,

My Son

Special Edition

A Blue Mountain Arts® Collection
of Thoughts Every Parent
Wants to Share with a Son

Edited by Gary Morris

Blue Mountain Press™
Boulder, Colorado

We wish to thank Susan Polis Schutz for permission to reprint the following poems that appear in this publication: "Remember These Things, Son," "Whatever You Choose to Do with Your Life, I Will Be Proud of You," and "My Son, Always Stay the Unique Individual That You Are." Copyright © 1991, 1994 by Stephen Schutz and Susan Polis Schutz. All rights reserved.

Library of Congress Catalog Card Number: 94-31218
ISBN: 0-88396-799-5 (hardcover) — ISBN: 0-88396-396-5 (trade paper)

ACKNOWLEDGMENTS appear on page 64.

Certain trademarks are used under license.
BLUE MOUNTAIN PRESS is registered in U.S. Patent and Trademark Office.

Manufactured in China.
First printing of this edition: 2004

 This book is printed on recycled paper.

This book is printed on fine quality, laid embossed, 80 lb. paper. This paper has been specially produced to be acid free (neutral pH) and contains no groundwood or unbleached pulp. It conforms with all the requirements of the American National Standards Institute, Inc., so as to ensure that this book will last and be enjoyed by future generations.

The Library of Congress has cataloged the softcover edition as follows:
There is greatness within you, my son : a collection of poems from Blue Mountain Arts.
     p. cm.
     ISBN 0-88396-396-5 (softcover)
     1. Mothers and sons—Poetry. 2. Fathers and sons—Poetry. 3. American poetry—20th century.
I. Blue Mountain Arts (Firm)
PS595.M66T48   1994
811'.54080920441—dc20
                                                94-31218
                                                    CIP

Blue Mountain Arts, Inc.
P.O. Box 4549, Boulder, Colorado 80306

Contents

Son, I'm Very Proud of You

*T*here have been moments when all I wanted to do was hold you in my arms and tell you everything would be all right. But as a parent, sometimes my job was more than just giving a reassuring hug.

I had to let you find out things for yourself, even when the outcome was painful. It wasn't always easy, but I believed it was necessary.

If I allowed you to think that any problem you ever had would go away just by wishful thinking, I wouldn't have been fulfilling my role as a parent. You had to learn and grow through your own trials and experiences — slowly but surely building self-confidence and courage with every step you took.

I encouraged you to be yourself, feel comfortable with who you are, and not let any obstacle in front of you frighten you away. I tried to teach you courage and positive thinking to guide you over uncertain waters.

I did the best I could with whatever tools I had. I wasn't a perfect parent, but I tried. And through all of the tears and the worrying, you turned out just fine. You're successful and intelligent, and there is no limit to where you can go or what you can do. But more than just your accomplishments got you to where you are today. Good morals, a sense of humor, and a loving heart contribute to the wonderful man you are.

I love you, and I want you to know how proud I am of you.

— T. L. Nash

Son, I Want You to Know How Much You Mean to Me

Sometimes I can hardly believe
that the man I see when I look at you
used to be my little boy.
Where did the time go?
How did the moments turn into years
that disappeared behind us
at such great speed?

I am in awe at the changes that
have taken place in you,
and sometimes it saddens me
because that part of my life is over.
Yet I also feel the happiness
and pride in having a son
who is all grown up,
and nothing can dull or dampen
the wonderful memories I have
of you as my little boy.

Even the rough times, the trying times,
and the overwhelming times
have sweetened through the years.
Memories of you still bring
laughter and delight,
a warmness of heart,
and tears to my eyes.
The pride I have in you
and the love I feel for you
have continued to grow,
much like you have.
You are even more precious to me now
than you were before.
If you could look inside my heart
and see the love there,
if you could feel its strength and depth,
then you would know that you
have fulfilled my life in ways
no other person ever could.

— Barbara Cage

I Want to Thank You for the Gifts You Have Given Me

In your lifetime, you have given me
far more gifts than I can count;
yet the ones I remember most are
the ones you gave from within,
often without even realizing it.
As a child, you gave me the gift
of allowing me to see the world
through your eyes, and finding beauty
I had overlooked before.

The many memories we've made,
the love you have given,
   and the love I have for you
are lifetime gifts.
I want to thank you for all
   you've given me,
and let you know that
   one of the greatest gifts of all
is the joy that has been mine —
   ever since the moment
      I first held you in my arms.

— Deanne Laura Gilbert

Remember These Things, Son

Always keep your many interests —
they will keep you
constantly occupied
Always keep your positive outlook —
it will give you the energy to
accomplish great things
Always keep your determination —
it will give you the ability
to succeed in meeting your goals
Always keep your excitement
about whatever you do —
it will help you to have fun
Always keep your sense of humor —
it will allow you to
make mistakes and learn from them

Always keep your confidence —
it will allow you to take risks
and not be afraid of failure
Always keep your sensitivity —
it will help you to understand
and do something about
injustices in the world
As you continue to grow
in your own unique, wonderful way
always remember that
I am more proud of you
than ever before and
I love you

— Susan Polis Schutz

To You, Son, with a Lot of Love

Sometimes we need
reminders in our lives
of how much
people care.

If you ever get that feeling,
I want you to remember this...

I love you, Son.

Beyond words that can even begin
to tell you how much,
   I hold you and your happiness
      within my heart each and
         every day.

I am so proud of you, and so thankful
to the years that have given me
so much to be thankful for.

   If I were given a chance to be
   anything I wanted to become,
   there's nothing I would rather be
      ...than your parent.

   And there is no one
   I would rather have
      ...as my son.

                    — Laurel Atherton

Always Believe in Yourself, Son, and Remember That Anything Is Possible

Believe in what makes you feel good.
Believe in what makes you happy.
Believe in the dreams
   you've always wanted to come true,
      and give them every chance to.

Life holds no promises
   as to what will come your way.
You must search for your own ideals
   and work toward reaching them.
Life makes no guarantees
   as to what you'll have.
It just gives you time to make choices
   and to take chances
and to discover whatever secrets
   might come your way.

If you are willing to take
the opportunities you are given
and utilize the abilities you have,
you will constantly fill your life
with special moments
and unforgettable times.

No one knows the mysteries of life
or its ultimate meaning,
but for those who are willing
to believe in their dreams
and in themselves,
life is a precious gift
in which anything is possible.

— Dena Dilaconi

You Are My Hope
for the Future

When I held you as a child...
it was like taking up in my arms
all of my hopes for the future.
I loved you so much then
that I felt my heart would break
with the pride and joy I felt.
I wondered then who you would become,
and you haven't let me down.
You are a person to be proud of.
You are sensitive, but strong,
with the courage to follow your own path,
to know and do what is right for you.

The love between us needs few words,
but is the foundation for all we give
by being there, by sharing time and effort,
by our talks, and by our caring.
I'm proud when you accomplish things,
but even prouder of the way you live.
Whether you win or lose,
you do it with integrity and humanity,
and I respect that.
From your own efforts, there has grown
a deep goodness in you.
I can wish nothing more
than that your life will hold a future
of happiness.

— Ruthann Tholen

I'll Always Care
About Your Happiness

I realize that it isn't always easy for you
to open up to me about your life
and matters you may consider
too personal to share.
Perhaps because we are parent and child,
there are natural barriers
that stand between us
and make it difficult for us to communicate.
I can understand how you may believe
that we are too different,
and our places in life
too far removed from each other,
for me to be able to understand you.
Yet it is because I am your parent
that I try so hard to understand.

I can't read your mind or claim to know
all that you feel and experience
at any given time.
Yet I can remember my own trials at your age.
I won't tell you that I have all the answers
or that I always know what is right for you.
But because I love you,
I care about your happiness and well-being.
Because I am your parent,
there is a natural instinct that urges me
to protect you from any harm or pain
and a strong desire to remain
a part of your life.
I would like for you to remember
that I am always here for you.
And during the times when you aren't able
or don't feel comfortable enough
to approach me,
simply remember that I love you.

— Katherine J. Romboldi

*T*here was always something special about you. The average and ordinary were never enough. You had to climb a little farther, reach a little higher. While some dreamed dreams, wishing they would come true, you worked hard making your dreams a reality. While others hoped, you tried, and most often succeeded. I wanted you to know how proud I am of all you have accomplished, of all you have become.

— M. Joye

Whatever You Choose to Do with Your Life, I Will Be Proud of You

It is so important
to choose your own
lifestyle
and not let others
choose it for you
Do what you want to do
Be what you want to be
Look the way you want to look
Act the way you want to act
Think the way you want to think
Speak the way you want to speak
Follow the goals you want to follow

Live according to the truths
   within yourself
and know that whatever you do
I am here to support you
and always feel very proud of you

— Susan Polis Schutz

Be Yourself!

*T*his is the best and only
person you can be.
Don't take away from your uniqueness
by trying to change it.
Being yourself leads to success.
Being someone you are not, to failure.
Use your time and energy
to make the most of who you are —
to build yourself up,
not tear yourself down.

BE YOURSELF!
Care about and consider the feelings
of those closest to you,
but don't allow others to tell you
how to think, feel, be, or live.
Only you have the right
to make these important decisions.

BE YOURSELF!
If others reject you,
don't be hard on yourself.
Their rejection has nothing to do
with who you are;
it has to do with who they are.

BE YOURSELF!
Be honest, because if you aren't,
it will be impossible for you
to feel good about yourself, and
for others to feel good about you.
Self-respect begins with honesty;
the respect of others comes
as a result of your own respect for yourself.

BE YOURSELF!
Accept yourself as being imperfect,
but not unlovable,
for your strengths
far exceed any weaknesses.
Embrace the goodness in you;
there is more there than you acknowledge.

BE YOURSELF!
You are a part of the universe,
not by accident, but by design.
You have a special place and purpose.
Trust your creator.
There's a star in the sky
with your name on it.
Claim that star and let it shine.
For you...
for others...
for a world whose survival depends on light...
let it shine.

— Nancye Sims

I Wish
for You, Son

I wish you a star to light your way
when you can't see what's ahead.
I wish you strong winds
beneath your dreams, lifting you up
and carrying you on.
I wish you prayers, strong and deep,
untying your cares
when the threads get tangled.
I wish you hope in tough situations —
a faith built on infinite power.
I wish you a harvest of moments,
memories, and good times.
I wish you sunshine amongst the clouds
and smiles that turn anguish to joy.
I wish you silence when words aren't needed
and all that it takes
to watch your cares drift away.
I wish you tomorrows as vast as the universe —
opportunities far beyond
what your heart believes.
I wish you love, lasting and giving,
and a happy heart —
every day, all year.

— Linda E. Knight

Don't Ever Give Up
on Your Dreams

*T*here may be times when you feel as if you have taken a million steps toward your dreams, and acted on your plans, only to find yourself in the same place that you began from. At times like this, you must not give up.

When you feel as if all that you have strived after and worked for has failed, you must continue on. Though you feel lost, bewildered, and alone, continue to believe in yourself. If you allow discouragement and doubt to blur your vision and wash away your dreams, then you will be left with nothing. Visualize your way beyond the detours, standstills, and obstacles.

You will realize your dreams. When someone has worked as hard as you have and taken so many productive steps in a positive direction, they will succeed. Whatever the hurt of the moment may be, it will pass. Tomorrow is always a new dawn. Today, you must pause, rest, catch your breath, and then look ahead. Each step will bring you closer to your dreams.

— Vicki Silvers

Work Hard, Son... but Have Fun, Too

It's important to be serious
about your goals,
but I'm hoping you'll also remember
the enjoyable side of life.
Include some time-outs in your
  busy schedule;
don't let life rush by.
I'm hoping your quests will be successful,
but I'd also like to see you
spending good times with friends,
making special moments,
and doing things you want to do just
for the pleasure it brings to your heart.

Do the things that make you happy
to be you;
you are living in a world filled
with opportunities for good things in life.
Stay as special as you are
and as filled with hopes and dreams
    as you are today,
but please keep that boyish grin in place,
and always remember to make special room
for happiness in your life —
the kind that keeps you in touch
with your friends, your dreams,
and the world around you.
I'm very proud of you,
and I'll always be wishing for
    your greatest happiness.

— Barbara J. Hall

Be the Best You Can Be, and Be Happy!

*T*hink of the future as a wonderful
   door opening into a promising new land.
Learn from the past,
   but do not let it determine your future.
Forget about any past mistakes.
Be glad that you are living in a world
   that is so full of opportunity.
Be optimistic.

Appreciate the fact that you have God-given
    talents and abilities that are uniquely yours,
and don't be afraid to use them.
Seek the advice and help of others,
but always remember that
    yours is the final word.
Make your own decisions,
explore your own self,
find your own dreams.
Be persistent; try not to get discouraged
    when things don't go your way.
Do all that you can to make this world
    a better place to live.
Be aware that life isn't always easy,
    but that given time and hard work,
    it can be everything you want it to be.
Most of all, be happy!
The future awaits you,
    and it's a wonderful time to be alive.

— MacKenzie Sinclair

Make Every Day of Your Life an Adventure

For some, life is an adventure:
an adventure of the spirit
and of the body.
Each new day
begins with wonder and anticipation
for the newness that the day will offer.
It will bring opportunities for
growth,
love,
passion for being, and
the inner search for understanding.

Each day is unique, like a solitary snowflake
searching for itself and its place among the
millions of snowflakes that
have ventured on ahead of it.
Each new day adds color to the tapestry
of a well-lived life
and music to a carefree soul.

Each new experience blends to create a life
of purpose and passion
that shines like a lighthouse, sending its light
miles out to sea to guide weary or lost travelers
home to safety and the meaning
of their lives.

We are all here for a very short time.
The plan of this universe offers its share of
surprises and twists of destiny that curse the timid soul.
But those who live life as an adventure welcome
these turns in the road and quirks of fate.
For them, each day is packed full of as many sights and
sounds and tastes and emotions as they can experience.

For some, life is drudgery. It reeks of sameness
and routine, gray skies, dull sounds, bland people,
and suppressed emotions.

We make our days; they don't make us.
To live a life full of
adventure, learn to laugh more,
feel more,
share more,
learn more, and love more.

— Tim Connor

Son, I Want to Give You the Gifts That Last Forever

I want to give you
the kinds of gifts that will last
your whole life through,
things that you just
can't put a price tag on.
I want to give you
the courage to
stand up for what you believe in;
a level head;
   a warm heart;
a sense of humor
to get you through any situation;
the ability to keep
growing and learning
as life brings changes;
a positive outlook for the future;
the love and support
of friends and family;
and the confidence
   and inspiration
to follow your dreams
wherever they may
   take you.

— Morgan R. Gray

*T*his I ask of you, my son —
That you strive to be all that you can be,
   yet never become a copy of another
That you realize your own unique qualities,
   and all that makes you special
That you open your eyes to the beauty
   in each day
That you reach out to others less fortunate
   than you
That, by giving, you learn the joy of
   receiving
That you let go of the sadness of the past,
   yet always remember the good moments
That you learn to accept life as it is,
   even with its problems and disappointments
For life is meant to be enjoyed
   and, at times, endured, but never taken
   for granted
Just be aware at all times
   that you are one special person,
   among all special persons
And do the best you can.

— Rhoda-Katie Hannan

When you dream, dream deep.
When you love, make it last.
When you have hopes, hold on
to them with all your heart.
Your possibilities are unsurpassed.

When you share, share completely.
When thoughts wander, let them soar.
When your wishes come up empty, don't
give up on them. Your opportunities might
be just behind the next door.

When you deal with difficulties, keep
your courage. When you awaken,
remember that each sunrise is brand new.
When you travel toward tomorrow, choose
your own direction. Your happiness will
always help to guide you.

When special feelings come your way,
let them flow into your heart. When
miracles try to find you, don't hide.
When special people come along, let
them know what a blessing they are.
Smiles begin way down, deep inside.

— Collin McCarty

Never Underestimate Your Abilities

You can do all you're dreaming of.
Don't let those little doubts appear;
dismiss them from your mind.
You're so strong and capable;
you're brave and willing, too.
You have so many reasons to succeed,
so much in your favor,
and so much going for you.
Don't minimize your keen abilities
or deprive your dreams
of great fulfillment.
Recognize your strengths.
Adopt a positive approach.
Assert your powers of positive thinking.
Stay in control.
Above all, think you can,
believe you can,
and most certainly you will!

— Barbara J. Hall

How Can You Measure the Value of a Man?

The measure of a man is not found in
the things he owns,
or what he's saved for retirement,
or even his accomplishments.

The true measure of a man is found in
his faith and in his heart.

It's found in the friends who stand by him,
the strength he displays under pressure,
the sensitivity he unashamedly expresses,
and his willingness to reveal vulnerability,
    even at the risk of being hurt.

And it's found in the truth of his words,
    the genuineness of his life,
    his unselfish actions,
    and the values he lives by.

Determine the measure of a man
    not by admiring his trophies
    nor by comparing him to other men
    either weaker or stronger.

Determine the measure of a man
    by how much you trust him
        and believe in him,
and by how much his life enhances yours.

— Craig Brannon

As You Go
Through Life, Son...

Don't forget your self-confidence. When you rise in the morning and prepare for the day, ready your strength, for you will always need it. Hang on to your convictions, for they are what make you different. Give yourself credit for being intelligent and capable.

Don't forget your compassion. When you look at yourself in the mirror, study your face carefully. Look for the courage to believe in yourself. Find the will to face the day ahead. Know that you are human and therefore capable of failing.

Don't forget your hope. When you are certain there is none left, look deep inside. There you will find faith in yourself and in those you love. There you will find belief that tomorrow will come. There you will find comfort in knowing that you are loved by those closest to you.

Don't forget your charity. When you feel that there could be no pain greater than yours, look around you. Recognize that someone before you has suffered greater. Know that someone after you will suffer more. Realize that pain is relative to everyone everywhere.

Don't forget your laughter. When reasoning fails you and logic drifts far away, look to your heart. It is there that you will find the humor in life and your ability to laugh out loud at yourself without fearing criticism. Remember that there is more medicine in a laugh than in a tear.

Don't forget who you are.
Don't forget the part that is humane,
the part that is hopeful,
or the part that is charitable.
And never forget the laughter.

— Chris Marie Perrin

In My Eyes, Son...

I see you standing
  as you really are —
powerful, sensitive, determined,
  and gracious.
I can see you achieving everything
  you choose to achieve.
I can see you being exactly
who and what you want to be.
Look through my eyes for an instant,
and you'll see yourself
conquering all limitations.
Look through my eyes,
and see who you really are
and what you are capable of.
You can accomplish anything —
  I know you can.

— Lea Marie Tomlyn

If Someone Asked Me to Define the Perfect Son, I Would Say...

"Search for a young man whose heart
   is as big as the Grand Canyon;
search for a young man who thinks
   only of others;
search for a young man who does
   a thousand good deeds each day
      while expecting nothing in return;
search for a young man who suffers
   and never complains.
And when your search is over,
   if you have found such a young man,
then rejoice —
   for you have found my son."

— Jeffrey K. Lucas

I Wish for You, My Son, the Greatest Things in Life

I wish you Love: unconditional
and unending.
I wish you Understanding:
an open mind, a caring heart,
and answers to all of your questions.
I wish you Determination:
to go after what you want, make it
work, and do the right thing.
I wish you Faith: to believe
in yourself, to trust your abilities, and
to keep on trying.
I wish you Peace: the ability to
forgive, calmness in stressful
times, and the comfort of love.

I wish you Fulfillment: enough time to
do what you enjoy, someone to share
the good times with, the ability
to recognize when something isn't
working, and the courage to move on.
I wish you Joy: a sense of humor, a
hand to hold, and pride in what
you do.
I wish you Gentleness: in touching,
feeling, and experiencing everything.
I wish you Goodness: honesty, integrity,
and loyalty not only from others,
but from within yourself as well.
I wish you Patience: in your actions,
your words, and your quest to become
all that you can be.

— Barbara Cage

My Son, Always Stay the Unique Individual That You Are

Men are told by society that
they must always be strong
They are told to block out
all sensitive, "unmanly" feelings
Men are told that
they must be leaders
they must achieve
they must succeed in a career
They are judged their whole lives
by the power they have
and how much money they earn

My son, I hope you will never
feel pressured by society
You should be free to think
and do whatever you want
and to act the way you feel at all times
You should cry when you want to
and laugh when you want to
You should just be
the outstanding person
that you are —
the person that I am so proud of
and whom I love always

— Susan Polis Schutz

It Is All Up to You, Son, to Make Your Dreams Come True

If you believe in your dreams, and work hard and long toward making them part of your reality, then more than likely you'll achieve whatever dreams you want to come true.

When you believe in something and focus your time and talents toward fulfilling that belief, then as time passes you will be continually traveling in the right direction. If you have a positive attitude about your life, you have almost everything that you'll ever need. Hope, faith, and believing in good things will lead you on the right path to happiness and success.

Challenges will come into your life, but the way that you perceive them will determine how positive or negative they will be in relationship to your life. If you accept a certain amount of disappointment, and strive to replace it with optimism and hope, then it will be a strengthening element in your life.

The simple keys to life are those that you, yourself, must turn. They are the ones that tell you to expect happiness as well as change, and to make the most out of every day. Be ready to make your dreams come true, because it is all up to you.

— Dena Dilaconi

Son, You Are the Artist of Your Life

You truly are a blessed individual in life. You are gifted with an endless array of wonderful talents and opportunities, and a strong awareness of the importance of being you.

Take the time to discover and explore your gifts. Experience them with your heart and soul. Feel the pleasure and wonder of their expression. Create your own moments, live with individuality, and be yourself.

Your gifts are yours. Own them and give them life, then share them with others. You may look to others for a better understanding of who you are, but do not emulate them for the sake of "fitting in." Justice would not be done if you were to live the life of another.

Your life is yours — an empty stage, a blank screen — with you as the artist. You are free to create what you want. Always remember the vast potential with which you have been blessed.

— Nancy Somers Dougherty

You have so many moments ahead of you, Son...
days that will bring new people into your life, and times that will bring new friends into your world.

Having had the wonderful pleasure of knowing you (since the minute you were born!) and appreciating the million and one things that are so wonderful about you...

I will always hope that the people who share your life are special, insightful people who realize how lucky they are to be in the presence of a present like you.

— Marta Best

When Problems Overwhelm You, Here's a Little Poem for You to Remember...
Carry On

Carry on as I would, Son.
Lay your problems down to rest.
Put all bad times behind you
and strive to be your best.

Carry on with confidence;
your hands now hold the reins.
Don't think your talents won't compare,
for my blood runs through your veins.

Carry on with honesty;
you know what's right and fair.
Just call on me when problems strike;
you know that I'll be there.

Carry on the dream, my son.
Let your conscience be your guide.
Remember when you feel alone,
I'm standing by your side.

— Shelley McDaniel

"You Can Go as Far as Your Dreams Can Take You"

If you can reach out, you can hold on.
If you can imagine, you can achieve.
If you just begin, you can continue.
Search within, and you'll find a reason to believe.

If you can get involved, you can make it happen.
If you can give, you will be rewarded with the taking.
If you climb, you can climb even higher.
Envision it; your success is in the making.

If you trust the winner within you, you will win.
If you can keep the courage, you will go so far.
If you follow your ambitions, your course will guide you
towards a ladder that you can climb to your stars.

If you don't put limits on yourself,
you can always keep striving.
You might amaze yourself with what
you discover you can do.
If you want to reach out for happiness,
don't ever forget these words:

You can go as far as your dreams can take you.

— Collin McCarty

In life, there will always be
many paths to follow;
I hope you always choose
the right one.

If you give
a part of yourself to life,
the part you receive back
will be so much greater.
Never regret the past,
but learn by it.
Never lose sight of your dreams;
a person who can dream
will always have hope.
Believe in yourself;
if you do, everyone else will.
You have the ability
to accomplish anything,
but never do it at
someone else's expense.
If you can go through life
loving others,
you will have achieved
the greatest success of all.

— Judy LeSage

Always Be True
to Yourself, My Son,
for There Is Greatness
Within You

Throughout your life, I hope you will always
pursue sensitivity and kindness
    as your chosen way.
Your sense of humor is wonderful;
    hold on to it.
Being able to laugh at the world
    will see you through many hard times.
Guard against bitterness and sarcasm;
    they can destroy you.
Be yourself; the world will benefit
    from your talent and your humor.
Search for people who love and
    appreciate you for who you are
and who encourage you to improve.
Don't be satisfied with less
    than all you can be,
for you have greatness within you.

— Bill Cross

I have loved
watching you go through life
as only a child can...
laughing, crying,
so sure of yourself,
and at the same time
so often full of doubts.
My heart broke for you
when life was unfair;
I would have shielded you
from pain and heartache
if you had let me.

I wanted to protect you,
but you needed to grow
into your own person,
so I had to let go of you —
a little at a time.
That was one of the hardest
things I've ever had to do.

Your childhood is gone now,
   and I still miss those
      wonderful times,
but I am so proud of
the adult you have become.
I love you,
and whatever paths in life
you may choose to embrace,
   my love will be with you...
and I will cherish you always.

              — Peggy Selig

My Son, Never Forget
These Ten Things...

Your happiness, health, and safety
mean everything to me.

No matter how old you get,
I will always think of you as my child
and love you as much as ever.

I enjoy being with you
and am very pleased at the person
you've turned out to be.

Your voice is one of my favorite sounds,
and your laughter always delights me.

You should always believe
that you are capable and worthy,
precious and unique —
   and act accordingly.

You have touched my heart
and made me proud
more often than you could imagine.

Memories of you are very dear to me,
and sharing special times and traditions
makes them all the more enjoyable.

You bless my life in so many ways,
and I am thankful for the friendship
that we share.

There is nothing you could ever do
to lessen my love for you.

Being your parent has given me
happiness to the greatest degree,
and warmth that fills my heart.
I am in awe that you came into my life
and made my dreams come true.

— Barbara Cage

Whether He's a Little Boy or a Grown Man... A Son Is Special

No one can drum up mischief
more quickly than a boy —
yet still look so innocent behind
a wide-eyed smile.

No one else can thrill your heart
    with flowers from
        your own backyard,
drawings done in crayon,
or his sweet attempts at trying
    to help out.

No one else can fill your home
    with laughter,
captivate your heart completely,
and make you happier day by day
    and prouder
as the years go by.

No one is dearer than a boy...
    except the special man
        that he grows up to be.

— Barbara J. Hall

ACKNOWLEDGEMENTS

We gratefully acknowledge the permission granted by the following authors, publishers, and authors' representatives to reprint poems or excerpts from their publications.

Katherine J. Romboldi for "I'll Always Care About Your Happiness." Copyright © 1994 by Katherine J. Romboldi. All rights reserved.

M. Joye for "There was always something special...." Copyright © 1994 by M. Joye. All rights reserved.

Nancye Sims for "Be Yourself!" Copyright © 1994 by Nancye Sims. All rights reserved.

Lisa Hellermann for "Don't Ever Give Up On Your Dreams" by Vicki Silvers. Copyright © 1994 by Vicki Silvers. All rights reserved.

Barbara J. Hall for "Work Hard, Son... but Have Fun, Too," "Never Underestimate Your Abilities," and "Whether He's a Little Boy or a Grown Man...." Copyright © 1994, 2002 by Barbara J. Hall. All rights reserved.

Tim Connor for "Make Every Day of Your Life an Adventure." Copyright © 1993 by Tim Connor. All rights reserved.

Chris Marie Perrin for "As You Go Through Life, Son...." Copyright © 1994 by Chris Marie Perrin. All rights reserved.

Jeffrey K. Lucas for "If Someone Asked Me to Define the Perfect Son, I Would Say...." Copyright © 1994 by Jeffrey K. Lucas. All rights reserved.

Dena Dilaconi for "It Is All Up to You, Son, to Make Your Dreams Come True." Copyright © 1994 by Dena Dilaconi. All rights reserved.

Nancy Somers Dougherty for "Son, You Are the Artist of Your Life." Copyright © 1994 by Nancy Somers Dougherty. All rights reserved.

A careful effort has been made to trace the ownership of selections used in this anthology in order to obtain permission to reprint copyrighted materials and give proper credit to the copyright owners. If any error or omission has occurred, it is completely inadvertent, and we would like to make corrections in future editions provided that written notification is made to the publisher:

BLUE MOUNTAIN ARTS, INC., P.O. Box 4549, Boulder, Colorado 80306.